THE LON

London - a playground of endless incredible experiences for those who put the effort into finding them.

Yet, when I ask people about their upcoming plans, they typically fall into one of three categories:

- get pissed at the local pub
- visit the trendy new pop-up plastered over every advertising platform
- see an overrated tourist attraction that every idiot has heard about.

There's seriously so much more to this city...

This bucket list contains 50 activities that will surprise and shock you with their awesomeness.

Whether you're a tourist, a student or a long-time resident looking to fall back in love with London, this is the bucket list for you.

Enjoy.

1. LADY DINAH'S CAT EMPORIUM

If there's a more tranquil way to enjoy afternoon tea than while stroking a friendly playful pussycat, I haven't seen it. London's original cat cafe serves a wide range of wonderful teas, coffees and light snacks all in the company of its nine friendly felines. Some of them are available for adoption, so let the staff know if you fall for one pussy in particular. Of all the quirky cafes in Shoreditch, Lady Dinah's may be the most in-demand, so book your 90-minute session in advance at ladydinahs.com.

Image credit: Instagram @dickjacksmith

2. DINO SNORES AT THE NATIONAL HISTORY MUSEUM

I've woken up to some surprising sights in my time, but nothing quite as startling as Dippy the Diplodocus. The National History Museum puts on quite a show for its bi-monthly sleepovers. Guests can enjoy a three-course meal, treasure hunts, live music and an all-night monster-movie marathon among other activities. You'll also have the chance to explore the galleries and exhibitions after the daytime visitors have gone home. See nhm.ac.uk to book tickets.

Image credit: Instagram @thianyenyee

3. CEREAL KILLER CAFE

Those who said it would never catch on certainly underestimated London's love of cereal. The UK's first speciality cereal cafe is now open in Camden and Shoreditch. With 120 cereals to choose from, you'll be spoilt for choice. What's more, there's 30 flavours of milk and 20 different toppings. To accompany that frantic sugar rush feeling from your childhood, the cafes are filled with 80s and 90s memorabilia. You can book private hire or a birthday party at cerealkillercafe.co.uk.

4. SILENT DISCO AT THE VIEW FROM THE SHARD

Looking for a Saturday night party spot that hits new heights? How about the top of Western Europe's tallest building? The Shard hosts silent discos on most weekends of the year. Once you arrive at the 800ft high arena, you'll be handed your wireless headphones connected to three competing DJs. Each will attempt to keep you tuned to their station with some epic party anthems. Fancy singing along to The Killers while your date dances to Dolly Parton? Head to timeout.com to book your tickets.

5. WEST END MUSICALS

If only London life was like a musical - we'd all walk down the streets with a skip in our step and a song in our heart. Whether you're sampling the multi-award winning Book Of Mormon, experiencing the unforgettable Phantom Of The Opera or being dazzled by Disney's adaptation of The Lion King, you'll leave the theatre grinning from ear to ear. There's a West End show suited to everyone's tastes so book a ticket now. My favourite website for cheap theatre tickets is getintolondontheatre.co.uk.

Image credit: Instagram @elstowbridge

6. GO APE

I'm not sure whether Tarzan would survive living day-to-day life in London, but he'd feel right at home at this forest adventure. This aerial obstacle course lets you swing through the trees as if you're king of the jungle. You'll fly down zip-wires, leap off sky-high swings and tackle some terrifying crossings. The crossings in Battersea Park are twice the height and length as those on other Go Ape courses. North Londoners can opt for the course at Trent Park instead. Book your treetop adventure at goape.co.uk.

7. ICEBAR LONDON

You've not tasted cocktails until you've swigged them from a glass made of crystal clear Swedish ice. This is literally the coolest drinking spot in central London. The walls, bar and tables are all sculpted from Sweden's purest ice source, the Torne River. The Mayfair venue is kept at a chilly -5C at all times, but you'll be given a thermal cape with a hood and gloves to keep you warm. Tired of the UK's tropical temperatures? Book your 40-minute visit at icebarlondon.com.

8. FIRE HAZARD GAMES

Credit to the Fire Hazard Games crew for turning our capital city's streets into an adventure playground. Their high-energy scavenger hunts take place all over the city. Feel your heart race as you become a spy, war survivor or action hero for an hour. Solve cryptic clues and avoid patrol guards to pass through as many checkpoints as possible. Compete with other teams and get text updates informing you of your position on the leaderboard. All games are affordable, enjoyable and easy to play. Choose from the list of missions at games.fire-hazard.net.

Image credit: Instagram @thatgirlb

9. WARNER BROS. STUDIO TOUR

A magical experience for Harry Potter enthusiasts. Pose for photos on Privet Drive and Platform 9 ¾. Jump on the Hogwarts Express. Ride broomsticks and taste butterbeer. Purchase all the merchandise you can imagine in the enormous gift shop. This tour is a movie nerd's delight. The audio guides are filled with facts, but the staff really know their stuff too. With so much to see and do, it'd be easy to spend three or four hours here. Book tickets at wbstudiotour.co.uk.

Image credit: Instagram @patasuciacontessa & @jdesignergirl

10. THE MAYOR OF SCAREDY CAT TOWN

A secret cocktail bar which needs a password to enter. It's like something from a C.S Lewis novel. Take your date to the Breakfast Club in Spitalfields and tell staff you're 'here to see the Mayor'. You'll be led through a Smeg fridge, down a darkened stairwell to a New York City inspired speakeasy. This candlelit den serves American diner style food and fabulous cocktails. Try the DIY Bloody Marys, which come with over 20 ingredients for you to add. More info at themayorofscaredycattown.com.

11. BOTTOMLESS BRUNCH

London is not only an unrivalled night out. It also offers a morning after like no other. Some of the bottomless brunches in this city will have your stomach singing as if there's no tomorrow. Bad Egg in Moorgate serves two hours worth of Bloody Mary, Frizzante or Mimosa with three breakfast meals for £35. One Canada Square in Canary Wharf offers free refills on all sorts of booze when you order a two-course breakfast for £40. For more fantastic breakfasts, see the list of restaurants at thelondondater.co.uk/hangovers.

Image Credit: Tom Gilfillan

12. HIP HOP KARAOKE

Fancy yourself as the next Notorious B.I.G or Nicki Minaj? Now is the chance to show the world how to drop some serious bombs on the microphone. Bobby Champagne Junior hosts this legendary evening every Thursday at The Social in Central London. The party goes on from 7pm all the way until 1am. It's a popular event so email your song requests to hiphopkaraoke@gmail.com and arrive early. As Eminem once said, 'you've got one shot, one opportunity to seize everything you ever wanted…'

13. ROCKAOKE

Have you always wanted to front a badass rock band but never got round to it? Rockaoke gives you the chance to do just that. Take to the stage and strut your stuff like a rockstar. Pretend you're Axl Rose with AC/DC or Adam Lambert with Queen. Or if you prefer, take on the likes of P!nk, Katy Perry, Pixie Lott etc. The three-piece band has an impressive repertoire of songs and play regular shows across London. See rockaoke.co.uk for more information.

14. ZOMBIE APOCALYPSE SURVIVAL

Do you have the skills to survive a Dawn of the Dead style zombie invasion? Hidden in North Greenwich, the decommissioned nuclear shelter Bunker 51 provides the best place to prepare for one. This SWAT experience involves training with three types of weaponry - airsoft, laser tag and paintball guns. Expect gore, big scares and plenty of blood as you battle to save the world from imminent disaster. You must be physically fit and ready to blow some zombie brains out! Book this exhilarating experience online at ultimaterecreation.co.uk.

Image credit: Instagram @ovo_hustler

15. CYBERDOG

This is quite simply the most fun shop I've ever set foot in. Come for the futuristic fashion, clubwear and rave clothing. Head downstairs for sex toys and fetishwear. Stay for the ear-splitting EDM music and podium dancers. I'd love to pop a molly, purchase some neon tights, then spend the rest of the day raving near the changing rooms. Cyberdog is based in the centre of Camden markets. You can't miss it. It's guarded by two giant steel robots and surrounded by delicious food stalls. Shop online at cyberdog.net.

16. EMIRATES AIR LINE

The UK's first urban cable car presents London like you've never seen it before. Soar through the sky at a height of 90 metres and take in the sights as you cross the Thames. Hop on and off at Greenwich Peninsula or the Royal Victoria Dock. The O2 Arena and ExCel London are among the attractions within easy access. It beats having your face crushed into another commuter's armpit on the Jubilee Line. A trip costs £3.40 on your Oyster card. Frequent flyers can purchase ten trips for £16.

Image credit : Paul Kohlhaussen

17. THE STAX BURGER CHALLENGE

There's something so inherently masculine about an eating challenge. The meat sweats. The stomach pains. The opportunity to claim a prize, and even have your photo immortalised on a wall of WINNERS. To compete in The Stax Burger Challenge, simply consume a five-patty beef burger, basket of fries and super-size milkshake as speedily as possible. The fastest time of the month wins dinner for two and a t-shirt, plus the chance to compete in the annual Ultimate STAX Burger Tournament. There's more info on that at staxdiner.com/#challenge.

18. HIPPODROME CASINO

The UK's biggest and busiest casino offers three floors of roulette, craps, blackjack, baccarat and slot machines. The award-winning theatre presents the best artists in jazz, swing, soul and cabaret every night. The Heliot Steak House serves fantastic food and cocktails at any time of day. Be sure to check out Lola's Underground casino, where the blackjack tables circle around caged burlesque dancers. Feeling lucky? Head to Leicester Square and hop inside. The Hippodrome is open 24/7 and no membership is required. More info at hippodromecasino.com.

19. PEDIBUS

Why choose between getting pissed up and sightseeing in the city? With the Pedibus you can do both. Bring your own booze and enjoy the view while party tunes blare from the speakers. Up to four Pedibuses (or 48 people) can travel along the same route. With a seating configuration similar to that of a dinner table, it's the most sociable form of sightseeing. Twice as cool as Boris bikes and fifty times more fun than walking. Book at pedibus.co.uk.

20. BOGAN BINGO

Bogans are defined in the dictionary as uncouth, unsophisticated Australians, but that doesn't mean they can't sort out a kick-ass game of bingo. In fact, these belligerent bogans have put it back on the map, so grab your balls and bingo markers and get ready for some bizarre, boozy fun. Expect cheap drinks, classic rock and crap prizes. Tickets for this weekly show, based at The Slug in Fulham, tend to sell out in advance, so book them now at boganbingo.co.uk.

Image credit: Instagram @jeromemaasphotography

21. REBEL BINGO

This is bingo on ecstasy. Expect foul-mouthed number calling, screaming, raving, glitter cannons, glorious highs and humiliating lows, all mixed with a wild, weird night of 80s and 90s anthems. Make sure to enter the venue early to get your ticket. If your numbers are called, sprint up to the stage and compete for the chance to win some impressively epic prizes. That's if you're not distracted by all the filth and tomfoolery taking place in the meantime. For details on upcoming events, get on the mailing list at rebelbingo.com.

22. KAYAK ALONG THE RIVER THAMES

Here's your chance to kayak across the UK's largest river. Paddle past the Houses of Parliament. Glide towards the London Eye. Get to Tower Bridge and stop for some well-earned snacks and drinks. Alternatively, take in the picturesque Ladbroke Grove and Little Venice. The kayaks are highly stable and guides will help you master the basics of boat control, so no experience is required. For a more romantic row, book your boat trip to coincide with the sunset. More info at kayakinglondon.com.

23. THE CIRCLE LINE PUB CRAWL

There are plenty of great London pub crawls that are guaranteed to get to you mortal. Check out the 'Monopoly pub crawl' or the official pub crawls taking place in Camden, Shoreditch and the City. I've never witnessed carnage like the Circle Line Pub Crawl though. The rules state that participants must imbibe one beverage at the pub nearest every stop on the Circle Line. That's 27 in total. Government guidelines prevent me from officially recommending it, but you can find out more at thecirclelinepubcrawl.co.uk.

24. THE JAZZ CAFE

This is one of London's most legendary music venues. Since opening in 1990, it's brought the likes of Adele, Amy Winehouse, Grandmaster Flash and countless legends of jazz to the heart of Camden. The recently renovated venue is looking fresher than ever and has a food menu that doesn't disappoint. If you love live music, book a ticket to see some of the capital's best soul, funk, hip hop and jazz acts. Discover upcoming gigs and order tickets at thejazzcafelondon.com.

25. PRIDE FESTIVAL

An epic celebration of LGBT culture in London. The two-week celebration culminates in tens of thousands of people gathering for the Pride in London Parade. The parade is a colourful carnival celebrating the diversity of our capital city. It welcomes people of every race, faith and sexuality. There's no street party like it. Many revellers dress in bright rainbow colours with plenty of face paint, make-up and glitter. The next London parade takes place on 1 July 2017. More info at prideinlondon.org.

26. WIMBLEDON

The world's most famous tennis tournament brings all of the sport's best players to South West London every year. A ground ticket gets you access to dozens of courts for the whole day. Some were available for less than £10 in 2016. You can queue for Centre Court or Court 1 tickets without pre-booking, but you'll have to camp in Wimbledon Park from early on in the previous evening. Alternatively, park up on 'Murray Mound' and watch the action on the big screen with a Pimms and some strawberries and cream.

27. MUSIC FESTIVALS

London provides unparalleled opportunities to listen to incredible live music. Its weekend-long festivals welcome some of the world's most well-known artists. If you're into commercial artists, book tickets for British Summer Time (Hyde Park) or Wireless Festival (Finsbury Park). Alternatively, enter the lottery for free tickets to the Apple Music Festival in Camden. Prefer your rock n' roll? Go for Calling Festival (Clapham Common) or Camden Rocks (various Camden venues). If you're more of a raver, you want SW4 in Clapham Common.

28. UP AT THE O2

Here's your chance to hike up the roof of one of the UK's most iconic live music venues. March up to the 170ft high observation platform for some spectacular views of the capital. Book a sunset or twilight session to witness the bright city lights shining in the night sky. It's a steep climb, but the instructors ensure even the most nervous 'urban mountaineers' ascend the arena safely. Many combine their climb with a trip to the O2's cinema or one of its restaurants. Tickets are available from theo2.co.uk.

29. LONDON SEVENS

Come for the rugby, stay for the carnival atmosphere. This fast-paced, high-scoring international tournament attracts huge crowds to Twickenham every year. With just seven players on each side, the matches are fast and furious. Nevertheless, the best thing about the tournament is the fantastic efforts that attendees put into their costumes. Fancy dress was banned in 2016 in an attempt to limit drunken tomfoolery, but it will be back next year following protests to The Rugby Football Union.

30. ESCAPE ROOMS

Team up with your smartest mates to solve puzzles and escape the room within one hour. Choose between escaping from a cursed Egyptian chamber or the clutches of an evil Chinese emperor. Based on the popular online game Takagism, both situations will test your teamwork, intuition and wit. Will you be able to escape without receiving any hints? You'll need to be physically wise to do so. One challenge features laser beams which you're penalised for breaking. Teams can consist of three to seven members. Book online at escaperooms.co.uk.

Image credit: Instagram @thetimothydrake

31. SECRET BRUNCH

On the surface, it's a fancy meal in a secret location. In reality, it's so much more. The Secret Brunch website invites you to rub shoulders with the 'well-heeled trendsetters of Europe.' It makes you apply for membership before buying a ticket. As pretentious as this sounds, you can definitely expect luxury, glamour and excess. No two brunches are the same. The creative team goes all-out on every single event, so purchase your ticket, wait for the theme to be announced, then prepare for one hell of a party. More info at secretbrunch.com.

32. CHESSBOXING

The self-proclaimed 'greatest sport in the world' is simple enough to understand. One round of chess. One round of boxing. Rinse and repeat until there's a checkmate or KO. London Chessboxing shows take place every few months. Attendees can expect DJs and cabaret entertainment, as well as the battles of brains and brawn. Keen to prove yourself as the world's strongest and smartest man? You can train to be a chessboxer at Islington Boxing Club every Saturday. More info at londonchessboxing.com.

33. LONDON COMIC CON

Comic book geeks of London unite! This convention celebrates everything awesome about anime, video games, comic books and cosplay. It's your chance to sample the latest releases, buy merchandise and meet celebrity guests from the world of nerd. Incredible fancy dress is heavily encouraged. London Comic Con comes to ExCel London twice a year, usually on the last weekends of May and October. It's one of the friendliest, funniest crowds you'll ever be a part of. Get tickets from mcmcomiccon.com.

34. THE PIANO WORKS

London's only non-stop live music venue - and it plays hits you won't hear anywhere else. The pianists only perform songs requested by the audience, so prepare to hear your favourite ballad play as you enjoy delicious food and drinks. Once the alcohol starts flowing, you can expect half the venue to sing along too. Based in a small Farringdon warehouse, The Piano Works outlines itself as part party, part bar, part restaurant, part club, part concert. One thing's for sure, it's a whole lot of fun.

35. BRENT CROSS BEACH

It's nowhere near the coast, but that's not stopping Londoners sunbathing on the beach this summer. The capital's biggest urban beach pops up opposite Brent Cross Shopping Centre between July and September. As well as 2,500 square metres of sand, you can enjoy street food, entertainers and an extensive family theme park. It's open every day until 10pm and entry is only £3. If Brent Cross is too far for you, make a trip to the urban beaches in Camden, Covent Garden and the South Bank instead.

36. MINISTRY OF SOUND

Situated in Elephant and Castle, this superclub is the home of electronic music. With its multi-award-winning sound system and event list littered with world-famous DJs, it's an essential spot for serious revellers. Every big-name DJ from Tiesto to Pete Tong and David Guetta has wowed huge crowds here. London's longest-running student night Milkshake takes place here every Tuesday. Students can also claim £5 off their cover charge on any other night. For sizeable discounts on entry fees, pre-book at ministryofsound.com.

Image credit: Richard Murgatroyd Photography

37. PROJECT AWESOME

Are you ready to wake up London with a power boost of positivity? London's most fun and friendly fitness movement is FREE, but it's not for the feint-hearted. Turn up at 06.30 at Tower Bridge (Weds) or Primrose Hill (Fri) ready for a badass workout. Commit to a class but fail to show up and you'll feature on the wall of shame. Still, if you love high fives, hugs, sweating and smiling, this will be the perfect start to your day. See projectawesomelondon.com.

Image credit: Instagram @emsifer

38. CIRCUS

You've not experienced fancy dinner until you've dined with pole dancers and acrobats performing just a few feet from your meal. The pan-Asian menu at this Covent Garden cocktail bar is beyond delicious, but it's the glamorously talented cabaret acts that make this a night to remember. The lengthy banquet tables double up as a catwalk for burlesque dancers and trapeze artists. Dinner and a show has never been intertwined so spectacularly. Staying late on the weekends? Expect party anthems and dancing on the tables. Book at circus-london.co.uk.

39. BUSK

Street performers are arguably celebrated in our capital more than anywhere else in the world. It's impossible to walk through the West End without being drawn in by energetic and accomplished buskers. Stumbling upon some musicians, beat-boxers or break-dancers is all part of the experience when exploring the city. It's super-easy to start earning money by showing off your talent on the streets of London. Look at buskinlondon.com for the rules, as well as an interactive map showing suitable locations to set up shop.

40. DANS LE NOIR

The truest definition of a blind date. At Dans Le Noir, you dine in total darkness, while being served by blind waiters and waitresses. Choose from one of four mystery menus (meat, fish, vegetarian, specials) before being led downstairs to dine. This unique experience will help you re-evaluate your sense of taste and smell – and there's something about complete darkness that makes you leave your inhibitions at the front door. All four menus are magnificent and you'll have a great time guessing what's on your plate. Book at london.danslenoir.com.

41. REGGAEROBICS

There's no shortage of unique fitness experiences in the capital, but this is definitely one of the most fun and dynamic aerobics classes around. The classes are based on African and Caribbean dance moves, as well as traditional aerobics exercises. You'll burn up to 750 calories per hourly session and pick up some eye-popping dance moves as you do so! Classes currently take place in Holloway on Tuesdays and Hampstead on Wednesdays, as well as at a host of day festivals. See twitter.com/reggaerobics for the latest information.

Image credit: (c) Mark Box flickr.com/photos/livinginaboxworld/sets

42. CHEAP NIGHTS OUT

A night on the lash in London need not cost an arm and a leg. I've compiled a 'Cheap Night Out Cheat Sheet' which lists tips for getting free entry and cheap drinks in some of the capital's best nightclubs. Did you know that Camden superclub KOKO runs a free club night on the first Saturday of every month, while tourist hotspot Zoo Bar often charges no cover before 23.00 if you sign up to its guestlist? For more money-saving tips like these, see thelondondater.co.uk/nightsout.

43. FREE STAND-UP COMEDY

When it comes to stand-up comedy, we're spoilt for choice in the capital. You can take out a second mortgage to see Michael McIntyre, Eddie Izzard etc at the O2 arena, but there's plenty of hilarity available across the city's dirt-cheap comedy clubs. For starters, there's the We Are Funny Project which runs free weekly shows in Putney and Dalston. Also, check out the Backyard Comedy Club in Bethnal Green, which hosts high-quality comedy at affordable prices most evenings.

44. THE CRYSTAL MAZE

You're not a true 90s kid unless you've fantasised about collecting crystals in the Aztec, Industrial, Futuristic and Medieval zones. Your team of eight will complete mystery, skill, physical and mental challenges, winning crystals to build up time in the Crystal Dome. You'll pay £50-£60 for the experience, but enthusiasts of the classic TV show will say it's worth every penny. Just don't be that idiot who gets locked in. Book tickets at the-crystal-maze.com.

45. BE ON TV

Some of the UK's favourite TV shows are filmed live in London - and you can be part of the experience by applying to be in the audience. Applausestore.com is a great place to start. Here you apply for the likes of Britain's Got Talent, X Factor, Top Gear and Take Me Out. Sroaudiences.com, lostintv.com and tvrecordings.com are all worth checking out as well. In many cases, it will cost you absolutely nothing, but you'll need to be lucky as there's nearly always more applicants than seats.

46. CHINATOWN

For an epic choice of Chinese takeaways, there's no better place to visit in the whole of the UK. Stroll through the delightfully decorated streets and choose from dozens of restaurants offering authentic Chinese cuisine. Skip breakfast and grab an all-you-can-eat buffet for less than £10. Check out the bakeries, supermarkets and souvenir shops too. My favourite is Four Seasons restaurant, famed for its Cantonese-style roast duck. Also, look out for Leong's Legend - the Taiwanese teahouse serving classic dim sum. Chinatown is situated just off Leicester Square.

47. HOT TUB CINEMA

This is less a cinematic experience, more an epic pool party with a film playing in the background. Book a tub with five friends - any less and you'll be sharing with strangers - then kick back while waiters ply you with food and booze. Once the film finishes, the staff fill the tubs with bubble bath and crank up the club bangers, but the crazy behaviour typically begins way before that. This is nothing like Netflix and chill. For screening times and tickets, visit hottubcinema.com.

48. BE A TOURIST FOR THE DAY

My main motive for writing this book was to encourage tourists to stray from the beaten path. But in truth, even if you live in London, it can be fun finding out about classic attractions such as Big Ben and Buckingham Palace. There's a free walking tour that sets off from Green Park every day at 11.00 and 15.00. The guides are always knowledgeable, enthusiastic and friendly, so tip them generously. Tourist hotspots like the London Eye, the London Dungeon and Madame Tussauds are all mildly entertaining too.

Image URL: https://www.flickr.com/photos/shardayyy/6556386319

Image credit: Flickr - Shardayyy (c) (edited)

49. WINTER WONDERLAND

If Santa Claus' sleigh was shot down by a bazooka, this is what his heaven would look like. There's fun and festivities as far as the eye can see. Take in the massive Christmas market, the exhilarating fairground rides, the fantastic food and booze in the Bavarian beer hall. Don your skates and throw some shapes on the ice rink. Take a romantic trip on the iconic Big Wheel. This is THE must-visit festive attraction in London. Head to Hyde Park any day from the end of November until the New Year.

50. BE ROMANTIC

The typical Londoner has no time for romance. We're all too busy and everything is so expensive. In spite of all the fantastic attractions featured in this book, most dates involve 'going for a drink' then wondering why it doesn't work out. Meanwhile, they're straight back on Tinder within minutes of meeting you because you did nothing to stand out. You know you can do better. Enter your email address at thelondondater.co.uk/dates and we'll send you seven unique London date ideas every Monday.

ABOUT THE AUTHOR

Joe Elvin is a magazine journalist who's been having the time of his life since moving to London in 2014.

Outside of the day job, he writes dating and self-development advice for the likes of Elite Daily, AskMen and Dumblittleman.com.

He shares a house in Tooting with four Australians, who are all as aspirational as him when it comes to hunting new adventures.

You can find the best of his blog posts at thelondondater.co.uk and stalk him on social media by following the links below.

www.facebook.com/joeelvinblog
www.twitter.com/LDNdater
www.instagram.com/thelondondater

21992426R00033

Printed in Poland
by Amazon Fulfillment
Poland Sp. z o.o., Wrocław